OLD GUY

JIU JITSU

Starting Jiu-Jitsu late, for Humans over 40

By

Eli Golub

Table of Contents

Dedication

This is for my amazing coaches and my teammates, without whom practicing jiu jitsu is imposssible.

Acknowledgments

My love and thanks to Lisa for encouraging me to take my notes to the next level, and to my parents and family, who have always supported me.

About the Author

Over 50 years of age, Eli Golub is a dedicated jiu jitsu practitioner who has been training since 2015. He is passionate about sharing his knowledge with others, particularly older athletes who are looking to stay active and challenge themselves. Eli has great respect for the art and its physical and mental benefits.

As a father of three, Eli brings a unique perspective to his writing and his book is a testament to his love of jiu jitsu and his commitment to inspiring others, regardless of age, to take up the sport. To connect with Eli and others, join the Old Guy Jiu Jitsu facebook group and check out Oldguyjits.com online.

△

Chapter 1: Start Now!

In my mid 40's, with three kids, a 50+ hour a week job in a foreign country, and with an impending divorce, I discovered Brazilian Jiu-jitsu.

It would not be entire truth to say it saved my life, as some claim, or that my transformation was immediate. Neither of these truths is strictly true.

But what is true is that no single physical pastime has done so much to better the quality of my life and affect me in so many profound ways, mentally, physically, and spiritually.

They say Jiu-Jitsu is for everybody. As a general statement, that's true. Jiu-jitsu is now more accessible than it's ever been, with really high-quality instruction to be found even in the most remote part of the world as practitioners of the art spread its reach all over the globe. It is suitable for all sexes and many physically other abled people. People with emotional and mental problems can also find great comfort in it. For people with difficulties in other parts of life, maybe marriage, home life, work, or social troubles can all be helped by being part of this group of people who can sometimes form another family around you.

In my case the effects of having this support were so significant, that I've decided to dedicate part of my life to helping others find that support. That's the purpose of this book. To support you as you make your way towards the mat, to present some answers to common questions, and help you stay training year upon year.

If you're reading this, then you're the segment of everybody that I also belong to. A guy or a girl over the age or close enough to the age of 40. You have special needs that younger humans don't have. Maybe you were an athlete in the past, maybe you spend your time walking, running, or biking, and that has gotten old as you have, and you're ready to try something new. Maybe you've NEVER been an athlete; that whole part of your childhood or teenage years was given over to other pursuits, and you're only now ready. It's said that it is never too late to start jiu-jitsu….until you are dead.

So start now. Get used to putting your excuses on the shelf and pushing through. Put down all the bullshit you're carrying through life at the edge of the mat, and escape into the flow. Make new bonds with other humans and start to learn how to improve yourself for optimal use out in the real world.

If you're already on Facebook, join the Old Guy Jiu Jitsu group, and look for more info over at Oldguyjits.com

Different things for different people

What does a father of five, an ambulance driver, a cop, a scientist, and a arborist all have in common? Not much at all, besides the fact that they are all verifiably human. As such, they have similar but not identical physical attributes. They've chosen to make part of their life the path of a warrior as much as society allows.

In most gyms, not all these people are "old." Nothing I'll present to you would be wrong for someone under 40 to adopt as a training methodology. But the things I'll share with you have been identified by myself and the community as being good choices to enhance the practice of an older martial artist.

Maybe you see yourself as old; maybe your kids and colleagues do. But people say age is just a number, and your feed is surely filled with people your age or older doing amazing things. Regardless of age, the thing jiu-jitsu people have in common is that all are a tiny bit (or a lot more) savage inside. An old savage can hang with a young crowd, but the way they go about it and their goals for rolls are much different.

Just starting

If you've never been to a single class, start on this page.

To train jiu-jitsu, you first need, above all, three things. I've listed them in a catchy little combo, but they're not in any particular order. You'll have to balance how important each is to you personally. A training situation will rarely be completely ideal. Compromises will usually be made. But generally speaking, what we're looking for is the quality of the Location, Lineage, and Look.

Location

When you're choosing a school, my philosophy is that you should find something as close as possible to where you spend most of your life. If you spend less time traveling, you can spend more time training or just living. For some people, this will still be a two-hour drive from something you could call a BJJ gym.

But generally speaking, search online right now for the three closest BJJ gyms to either home or work, depending on when you think you want to train and what your work schedule will allow. Imagine how you are going to fit this training into your day a few times a week, at least 2-3, as consistency plays a major role in your long-term success. Bonus points for finding three gyms that are strictly Brazilian Jiu-jitsu gyms and haven't added a BJJ program to supplement the Aikido, Taekwondo, or karate programs.

You will find, given its current popularity, a lot of karate or other martial arts clubs have added jiu-jitsu to their curriculum, but they are not jiu-jitsu schools. Second place in your ranking would be an MMA gym; these typically combine Jiu-Jitsu with Muay Thai and have dedicated instructors for each, with a focus on real sparring and practical application, as opposed to learning Kata and demonstrating flips and board breaking. Depending on your location, some of these gyms might also have a wrestling coach.

As a side note, a lot of practitioners find themselves eventually choosing work based on free time available for training. The extreme version of this would be actually working as a coach, working admin at a club, or training private clients.

So you've chosen the best two of those three gyms close to you. If there isn't a standout characteristic that makes one better than the other, like the quality of the facility or instruction, then you should schedule a trial at both. But typically, one of the gyms will remain as having the best balance that looks like it will work for you. Both Google Maps and Facebook are tremendously valuable tools to help you find the right club near you. Lurking a local gym's page, using maps to find the three closest clubs to work, home, or school, or stopping by the Old Guy Jiu Jitsu FB group for advice can help you if you get really stuck between choices.

Lineage

Check the website or the walls near the front desk. It should be crystal clear where your potential instructor learned their jiu-jitsu. In other words, they will list who awarded them their black belt and, usually, their entire jiu-jitsu family tree. This is called the lineage and has their instructor, instructor's instructor, etc. Usually, this concludes with Helio Gracie, Carlos Gracie, or the head of one of two or three other original Brazilian families developing the art.

As a single person or group of people that you will learn your technique from, the relationship between student and coach is a very important one. This is a good time to listen to your gut. If you get a bad vibe from your coach during your trial, or you see or experience something that gives you pause, make a note of it. Don't blindly sign up somewhere you think you might not like unless you have no alternative. In that case, you get what you get and make the most of it.

On the other hand, you aren't required to pay and train anywhere you don't like, ever, and you don't have to come up with elaborate excuses for why you don't want to continue training. Keep in mind that I am talking about legitimate complaints. If you don't like the coach because he makes you work hard enough to be sore, tired, or uncomfortable, you're likely missing the point. No club will be the right one to train at if this is your attitude.

I said in the beginning, put aside your excuses. You will learn to recognize the difference between a legitimate pause in training to resolve a serious injury or paying too much attention to "your inner bitch" (credit comedian Joe Rogan). All clubs worth trying have a free trial; they don't try and fool you, trick you, or trap you into an agreement. A legit club will tell you exactly what your agreement with them will be and what your financial obligations are. Clubs will often allow you to pause paying your membership for a specified time to allow for injury or extended absence (vacation, work trip, or injury). In my opinion, the best clubs have no contract, and if you want to leave, you can.

Depending on how far from population centers you're located, your instructor may have had a long road to get where they are, and sometimes you will find quality instruction by lower belts in remote areas. In any case, you should be able to easily tell its legitimacy. If not, then ask. You can learn great jiu-jitsu from a lower-ranked person who doesn't have a lineage. But that's likely an exception and not the rule.

Having a legit lineage will protect you from being taught what we sometimes call "Bullshido." This is a word derived by combining 'budo' (the art of war, or the code that all martial arts supposedly follow) and.... uh, Bullshit.

A legitimate coach will be happy to share their background with you, and if they are a competitor, a Youtube search should show you a good collection of matches. This is also a good place to check their style. For someone who is just starting (and also older people), the best instructors are often smaller males or females. They have had to evolve a game that uses much more technique and relies less on strength or size, attributes that we can plan on having less of as the years pass.

Look

How your future gym looks when you visit is the best indicator of what it will be like when you train there. Many BJJ gyms also house other sports or are an offshoot of the main training program. The mats don't rest, and you will be in constant contact with them. As hectic as the program at a gym is, they should be able to tell you exactly when cleaning staff are sanitizing the gym, and it should be clear that the place is maintained and kept clean.

The world is an increasingly unclean place, and you need to protect your health by training somewhere clean. It's almost impossible to avoid some kind of unique funk in the air of a gym, but there are levels to this. A shower is nice, and if there is one, it should be clean. Toilets should be clean, and there should be ample signage reminding people not to bring shoes on the mat.

On the subject of signage, the image and logo of the gym you choose probably should be something you can live with, much like a tattoo. I'm cool with it if you wear a t-shirt with a rabid mongoose on it if you are.

An affiliate is a satellite gym. These can run the full range from being part of a global organization like Gracie Barra or 10th Planet, or it could be just three local gyms that let their members cross-train between locations.

△

Chapter 2: The Gi

There are, broadly speaking, two types of jiu-jitsu being practiced out there. The first is "Gi," or regular Brazilian Jiu-jitsu. The Gi is a cotton or hemp canvas suit, a type of kimono. It is usually of lighter construction than its cousin, the judo Gi, but heavier than a karate gi and will be marketed specifically for BJJ. You can use a judo gi to practice jiu-jitsu, but it is typically made of heavier canvas. However, in a sport where most temperate climate gyms don't heat much, the judo gi can be great for training in winter. If you train somewhere excessively warm, you may want to avoid that, choosing a lighter weight ripstop gi instead, or training primarily no-gi (more on that below).

Keep in mind, if you will be focusing on competition that there are specific standards for garments in competition, and these are different depending on what ruleset you are competing in.

Below is the link address for the uniform info page of the IBJJF, one of the larger competition organizations. There are specific rules for the loose fit of pants and sleeves, correct lengths of the same, placement of patches, etc.

Ibjjf.com/uniform

IBJJF Uniform

If you compete at an event like this, your Gi may be checked on the day for the correct fit. Remember, your fighting weight is often WITH the gi on! That means you'll wear it on the scale.

Men's and women's kimonos (gi) are designed differently. Usually, a female gi has more room in the chest and hips, and a lot of the pants are cut a bit shorter. Unisex gi sizes are designated by the letter A for adults, followed by a number. So A0, A1, A2, A3, etc., up to 4 or 5.

Female sizes are often designated as F0, F1, F2, F3, etc.

Children's sizes are often the letter K or M

ALL gi sizes can have modifiers, depending on the manufacturer's labeling policy. So an A2 that is long will be an A2L, which has long sleeves and legs. An F2H might be a women's husky size, giving more room for people who don't shop easily off the rack. Some companies make just pants in every conceivable size[1], and there are a couple of companies that make completely customizable gi, including embroidery[2].

To put it in perspective, I am male, 165 lbs (75kg), and 5'11" (180cm). I fit in almost any A2 pretty easily, and I'd say it's the most common size for a guy. But between

---

[1] justgipants.com

[2] Killer Bee Gis

manufacturers, I can easily do an A1L, an A2, and an A2L, and I've even had an A3 jacket that fits me great.

If you buy your first gi and it fits you perfectly, and you love it, you win. But probably your taste for what's comfortable will change as you learn what suits you. My very first gi was an A4 judo gi. I thought it fit me pretty well in the shop, a huge martial arts market warehouse manned by a Greek guy who was a boxer and knew nothing of Brazilian jiu-jitsu. It was fine for my first few rolls with a friend[3]. But halfway through my first real practice, as I started to sweat, it kept getting bigger and bigger until my hands were buried halfway up the sleeves, and I started tripping on the pants hems. I ended up gifting it to my academy for all the big fellas to wear on their first day as a loaner. This brings me to loaners. A lot of gyms have them. If they don't, you can try a class or two in a pair of sweatpants or shorts. No pockets (finger breakers) or zippers (mat tears) allowed, and try and borrow a jacket until you buy one. Often another club member will mention at the end of class that they have an old gi for you to borrow or buy. I'm too addicted to buying myself a new gi every now and then to buy a used one, but I haven't seen one I like yet. It could be that one perfect gi somebody

---

[3] Which incidentally, was in the 4th story gym of a cruise ship at sea, with the floor rising and falling due to mounting waves, and my friend eventually puking in a trash can. We were ejected by the Hungarian bodybuilder that ran the place, who was furious we'd moved all his benches aside to make mat space.

wore once and decided it was a hassle to return. Gi is like jeans, you love them to the point that they break. Sure, you can get by with only one Gi, or if you want a little break from laundry every so often, two. I only have seven, and a few were gifts from my Mom, who is still a great cheerleader. Maybe ten, now that I think about it. But that isn't the point.

Your belt, when starting, will be a white belt, and it will be a whole size that corresponds with the gi size. So even if you are an A3L, your belt will just be an A3. The belt is part of the uniform and should be washed regularly. Don't believe any 'Bullshido' about the belt holding all your Kwan energy or the trapped souls of all the opponents you submit. The only thing the belt holds onto between practices is bacteria. Wash it with your GI!

In the US, you can get a good starter gi online for $100 or less. Prices internationally will be 1.25 - 2x+ unless you buy a domestic brand. Almost all the gi in the world are made in Pakistan or China. Origin Maine is a US-made brand, and a few other countries do have a domestically made gi. Don't pay too much for a used gi. It isn't being worn as a primary gi for a reason, but it will do for you until you figure out if you're going to stick around.

A lot of people don't stick around, which means there are a lot of gi out there on eBay that have only been worn a couple of times and then hung in the closet until the owner decided to accept they weren't ever going back to class. If you're looking at a couple Gi and can't decide which to get, come to the Old Guy Jiu Jitsu Facebook page and ask someone.

NOGI

In Brazil, jiu-jitsu goes hand in hand with surfing. Legend has it that challenges would spill out of dojos and onto the beach, or surfing disputes in the water would be brought to the sand to be resolved. Whatever the origin, the second (equal billing, though!) uniform and style in our sport are called no-gi. True to the name, you don't wear the kimono.

But you don't practice naked either, although pretty close. Imagine what a surfer wears, and you'll have a great idea of what you can wear for nogi. Typically it is a pair of shorts similar to board shorts. Usually, they have a string and velcro closure in front with no pockets or zippers. Try and find a pair that has a nice front waist. A lot of them have the edge of the velcro hanging out right across your belly, and it can be irritating.

I wear what are called spats under these; these are just tights. Compression wear is great to wear under the shorts, as they'll keep your privates private if your shorts get pulled off. I also find it gives me peace of mind against infection.

If you have bare flesh and get a scratch from a fingernail or toenail, it's easier to get infected from the mat. Having one more layer of fabric actually helps a lot. Also protects your knees and elbows from mat burns and some bruising. Depending on how casual your club is, some people roll nogi with no shirt on, but that's something you either see in the second half of practice on a sunny day or in a super fight. Otherwise, it's common to wear a rashguard up top. This often has a rubber hem to keep it from riding up too much while you roll.

You can get them in short or long-sleeved versions. Keep in mind that these are sold in "Ranked" versions corresponding to belt level as well, so make sure if you buy a ranked one, it is at least 10% white, as you will be a white belt when you start. If it is another color, that color should NOT be Blue, Purple, or Brown. Other colors are allowed, but the intention is for it to be clear what belt rank you are when competing without wearing a belt! Purple and brown ranked rash guards are always on sale, so unless you want to wear it once, be embarrassed, and then stick it at the back of a drawer for ten years, don't buy one of these.

△

Chapter 3: First Class

OK.

You found a place to train.

You met your coach.

You signed up.

You got a gi, or something suitable to wear.

Your trial class is tomorrow.

Pack your bag with what you'll wear. As you train more, you'll find a routine and habits for packing your bag.

What works for me is getting the bag ready to go again as soon as I get home from practice. This means dirty gi and rashguards (and belt at least every other practice) right into the wash to get clean right away (Don't let a dirty gi bake in the back of your car or lay in a pile in the corner if you can avoid it). Once the bacteria get into it, you can't ever really get it to smell good again. Then I put a clean gi and rashguards, towel, etc. in and fill my water bottles back up and chuck the bag back in the car, even if the practice isn't for a day or two.

A towel and knee or ankle braces if you need them. Carry a couple of pairs of spare underwear and a t-shirt. You can go to the chemist or pharmacy and buy a cheap boil-and-bite mouthguard that will only take you a couple of minutes to fit in your own kitchen. A lot of people don't wear a mouthguard for training, only for competition. A lot of dentists drive really nice cars. Make it a habit early to wear it when you live roll, especially if you'll be competing, as it takes some getting used to when you have to breath around a mouthguard.

Have a pretty big water bottle, and make sure you hydrate the day before and the day of. I can't stress this enough. You will sweat more than you thought was ever possible, and it will affect your performance. If you sweat a lot normally, you may want to put some salt or electrolytes in your water, especially if you sometimes get cramps. Try and avoid caffeine before practice if this is the case.

As you get deeper into the sport, you might get invited last minute to another gym or a friend's house to have a roll. If the bag is already packed, and in the car, you've already beaten an excuse. A lot of the secret of consistency is to not give your excuses a place to get comfortable. Consistency is key to progress.

Washing your used gi immediately prevents any funky bacteria from getting a foothold and will keep everything from stinking down the track. Unfortunately, many gyms have a person whose gi smells like cat piss. I could almost write a book on laundry now that I've been practicing jiu-jitsu for a few years, but try and keep it simple. I use dry powder and a liquid antifungal product in a cold wash. Hang everything dry.

A gi should almost never be dried in a hot dryer; this will cause it to shrink. Note that you can use this as a legit technique to shrink a large gi intentionally, but it's a one-way trip and NOT REVERSIBLE. To do this, you dry it as normal in a dryer but take it out periodically and check the fit. You will only be able to make it get a certain percentage smaller, and then it will stop. When you have checked until it's the fit you want, stop drying it and hang it dry. After this, wash as you would your other gi. Cold water, hang dry.

Your Gym Bag

Some savages show up with their rumpled (hopefully clean) gi in one hand, belt dragging along the sidewalk, and toothbrush in mouth. They sometimes forget a mouthpiece and usually have to borrow a pair of nail clippers. Don't be that guy. Be ready to train. Your gym bag should always have everything in it and be ready to go by the door. When you leave the house, it should be in your car.

Not having a bag packed or not having a gi ready in your car can be a major obstacle to your training, depending on how good at excuses you are. If it's good to go all the time, that means you are good to go. Don't forget, whatever other reasons you are training; the broad idea is to be always ready for a physical challenge.

In an extreme case, that is someone unexpectedly using force against you. But the other end of the spectrum of that is always being ready to visit another gym to roll with friends, pick up a competitive match at the last minute when somebody drops out or hit a practice you didn't think you'd be able to make until a hole in your schedule opened up.

So what's that stuff? What goes in your bag? In my bag, the general load that's always in there consists of some things that are a must and some that are for my own comfort. Obviously, you need to wear clothes when you train, and the main purpose of the bag is to keep together Gi jacket, pants, and belt. That is the bare minimum. I also carry a full set of No gi. That way, whatever style other people are practicing, I will be able to join. Depending on the season, I vary the length of the compression gear or rashguards I wear under my gi.

In winter, usually a long sleeve rashguard top and long tights (spats) on the bottom. This can really cut down on the number of skin abrasions and marks you otherwise get on your body as people grab your skin often through the gi. There is anecdotal evidence, and it is the general opinion that this extra layer can also give a bit of extra protection from skin infections you might get from the mat.

In summer, I usually wear compression shorts that are bike shorts length and a short sleeve rashguard under my Gi.

Actual nogi wear is kind of all over the map. You can wear any of the things described above without the gi over it. Most guys usually wear MMA fight shorts as well, either by themselves or over rashguard bottoms for modesty. Some people practice Nogi with no shirt, only shorts. Many gyms do not allow this, and relatively few females want to roll with someone with no shirt, although standards will vary widely depending on local weather and cultural attitudes. The minimum in a professional fight could be something called Vale Tudo shorts, similar to what pro wrestlers wear. Anytime you travel and are planning on visiting a gym (and I highly recommend you do, it is really rewarding), you should have a rashguard (and Gi obviously) with you, whether you normally wear one or not. You should also try, when possible, to bring a white Gi without club markings and minimal patches. Clubs have different rules on this, but it would be a drag to travel to another country and not be able to train for such a silly reason. When in Rome…

Your bag should also carry your mouthguard, a water bottle, and a small towel. I also carry a toothbrush, deodorant, nail clippers, band-aids, and some kind of antiseptic cream. A little bit of money for a coffee or some food with your training partners. Personally, I love the micro fiber backpacker's towels that you can buy everywhere now. They dry super fast and pack very small. Don't buy a red one unless you want to accidentally dye your white gi pink. While I'm on the topic, usually not a good idea to bleach your gi in the wash.

Etiquette and Cleanliness

You will need a pair of flip-flops, slides, thongs, or shoes that you can slip on in case you need to use the toilet during practice. You should be barefoot on the mat and use shoes as soon as you leave it; this keeps the mat as clean as possible and hopefully prevents nasties from migrating onto the training area. Never, ever go into the toilet area without shoes on.

Hair, Breath, Body, Nails

You will be spending a lot of time in really close proximity to the people you train with. As such, you should always be really conscious of the impression you are making with your appearance, but also how you smell. Some of this was covered in the laundry section, but it's up to you to make sure you are presentable.

This means if you are a smoker (and you can still get anyone to roll with you), you should have washed your face and hands, changed out of whatever clothes you were wearing when you smoked and brushed your teeth so that your partner doesn't feel like they're sucking on an ashtray for the whole practice. It's a good idea anyway to keep a spare toothbrush and toothpaste in your gym bag.

While we're on the subject of smoking, jiu-jitsu has an entire subset of practitioners that love cannabis. All judgment aside, whatever works for you, maaaan. But don't be so twisted that you show up with glazed eyes and can't follow the instructions of your coaches, some of whom will not be amused at all. This is usually for people who have some idea of what they're doing on the mat. This will not likely be you for several years after you start. Don't handicap your ability to learn right out of the gate, and be aware that there are widely varying standards for this, depending on your club. While Eddie Bravo's 10th Planet affiliates almost consider it a prerequisite to roll stoned, arguably, the vast majority of common clubs may look down on it. This depends not only on what country you're in but what part of the country. Generally speaking, if you are of this variety, your people will find you, or you'll find them, and neither will have to look very hard.

If you have long hair, it cannot be loose for practice. A ponytail is ok, but cornrows or tight braids are better. It should be clean and not greasy or smell bad. The hair at the back of your neck will take a beating, if it is long, from people reaching under your neck from the side or top control. Jiu-jitsu people often get sick of hair, and you'll see various people shave it off from time to time. If you have long hair, put an extra package of elastics or whatever you tie up with in your bag. Girls often braid or plait long hair to keep it out of the way or from being tugged on too much by the action.

If you are accustomed to dying your hair or wearing a lot of makeup, make sure the dye is well set and rinsed well. Remove makeup completely before rolling, even if your crush is likely to be there for practice. Both hair dye and makeup can ruin someone else's nice white gi, or worse yet, the mats, and it doesn't endear people to you.

If you're coming straight from work, you might not have time for a shower before practice, and for the most part, people are understanding. But if you're coming from home, take the time to hop in the shower or be acceptably clean before practice. Everyone expects you to smell by the end of practice, but no one will like it right at the beginning. Deodorant in the bag for emergencies or a little extra help.

Make sure you trim AND file your finger and toenails at least once a week. Untrimmed nails are a big danger to other people, and in the scuffle, you could give someone an easily avoidable skin injury.

The best-case scenario is this wound will take a long time to heal and be an annoying inconvenience every time they practice. Worst case, it leaves an open route for serious infection. So trim your nails well. Once they are trimmed, use an emery board or nail file to round off the sharp edges remaining. Rub your fingertips over all your nails and smooth any part that catches. Keep in mind any nail polish should have ample time to set up before you go on the mat, so a high-speed move won't leave a streak of nail polish on the gym mats. Cheaper polish is more likely to mark the mat.

If you typically sweat a lot, or this is early in your trip to get back in shape, you might need a towel. A small towel is great to have in your bag to keep at the edge of the mat with your water.

Take time for good Warm Ups

A younger player can show up at the time practice is meant to start and quickly change, run out onto the mat, slap hands, and start. This does not suit an older grappler at all and is a common route to injury.

It's crucial that the older practitioner takes the time to warm up properly. The warm-up should gently prepare the body for exercises by gradually increasing the heart rate and circulation. This, in turn, will loosen the joints and increase blood flow to the muscles. Stretching the muscles prepares them for physical activity and prevents injuries. The warm-up is also a great time for you to prepare yourself mentally for the fight ahead. Anxiety plays a big part in most people's jiu-jitsu journey, and it's totally normal to feel nervous in anticipation of physical conflict, especially as a beginner who has not normalized to the training. Warm-ups can also be used to practice solo skills and partner drills.

So warming up, above all, does three important things for us.

First, it helps prevent injuries, which is really important for us 'geriatrics.' Warming the muscles up works them through a full range of motion and gets them ready for sport-specific movement. Checking the full range of motion of each part of your body can help you identify problem areas or parts of the body that require you to modify your style to protect them when you roll. Injuries take much longer to heal as you age. It's common sense that the best way to keep injuries from affecting your practice is to not have any in the first place.

The second thing a good warm-up does is offset inflammation, which is a big challenge for an older athlete. I'll write a bit about inflammation later, but in a nutshell, there is ample evidence that stretching and passive recovery can help manage it. A good warm-up offsets inflammation because the muscles are not shocked with physical exertion straight off the bat. They have a chance to gradually get accustomed to movement, and this can help avoid hamstring tears or shoulder issues and the like.

Last but not least, warm-ups aid in flexibility, more specifically in maintaining it. Having great flexibility is only a natural physical attribute for a select few humans, and they are rare. Everyone else has to work at it, but everyone can improve it. For me, the single biggest factor in improving my enjoyment of jiu-jitsu was improving flexibility, which I personally do through the practice of yoga.

For every part of this warm-up, use the smallest range of motion first and build up to the full range. For some people, this will be as simple as working the full range of motion for every joint from the top of your head to your feet. A pretty full list of these motions are below. I'll repeat, as an older athlete, you need more time to warm up. So do them slowly. Don't rush through, or it's the same as jumping straight into practice. Generally speaking, if you warm up everything in order, the BARE MINIMUM should go something like this:

Neck

- 10x Ear to shoulder - each side
- 10x Slowly Nod Head Yes - full range
- 10x Slowly Shake head No - full range

Shoulders

- 10x forward rotations - keeping your palms flat against your thighs and your arms relaxed and straight, make a circle forward with your shoulders
- 10x backward rotations - as above, backward
- 10x small circles forward, arms outstretched
- 10x small circles backward, arms outstretched
- 10x large circles, as above
- 10x large circles, as above

Elbows

- 10x elbow rotations inward - keeping elbows near the body, windmill forearms in front of the body
- 10x elbow rotations outward - as above

Wrists

- 10x wrist rotation outward - with arms straight at waist height and hands flat, circle the thumbs outward
- 10x wrist rotation inward - with arms straight at waist height and hands flat, circle the pinkies inward

Fingers

- 10x Fingers - Extend all fingers like you are showing someone you have ten of something. Make fists with both hands. Repeat 10x like you have flashing lights for hands.

- Classical guitarists have a lot of great routines online for finger and wrist warm-ups and stretches

Hips

- 10x Hip Rotation Clockwise - Imaginary hula hoop. Slowly.
- 10x Hip Rotation Counter Clockwise - As above. Slowly.

Knees

- 10x Knee rotation - with feet together, bend both knees and place hands on kneecaps for support while your kneecaps make a clockwise vertical circle
- 10x Knee rotation - the opposite direction
- 10x Squat stretch - Place hands on the floor in front of feet, bend knees to a full range of motion and straighten.

Ankles

- 20x Right ankle Rotation - balance on left foot, raise right foot in the air and rotate clockwise 10x, counter clock 10x
- 20x Left ankle Rotation - balance on Right foot, raise left foot in the air and rotate clockwise 10x, counter clock 10x

- Sometimes I put the circling foot forward for the first ten and in the air behind me for the second ten. This wakes up your sense of equilibrium as well as dynamically engages the muscles in your other leg.

These warm-ups are intended for you to do BEFORE class starts. Be early to give yourself enough time. There are warm-ups in the beginning of class. These will be in addition to the above. Yes, you will often be warming up twice. Yes, a lot of students skip the warm-up or half-ass it. You're old, or you wouldn't be reading this. Stretch extra.

A great resource for stretching routines is youtube. There is an infinite variety; I would just say find something you like, that isn't too long, that you enjoy (or will do at least) and do it often. It will greatly enhance your enjoyment and advancement in the sport. GMB (Gold Medal Bodies) can do no wrong, and all of their videos are excellent in this area.

Keep Focus On Your Training

Training time is sometimes difficult to protect for the older grappler. By this stage in life, most people have work, family, and other obligations. Getting 2-6 sessions per week for a hobby away from home or work is sometimes hard to guarantee. So when you get it as an older athlete, maximize your time. Younger students might slack off during drilling or spend practice socializing. You don't have that luxury. Be mentally prepared for your session and pay attention. Other students your age have had to fight their own obligations and make personal sacrifices just to get to the mat; you should believe they are taking their own training commitment seriously, and you should be ready for them when you meet them in the crucibles of competition or training.

△

Chapter 4: Choosing partners

A few gyms will not let you 'roll live,' or actually wrestle anyone at first. They will take a few weeks or months to let you acclimatize, and then the coach will handpick the people for you to fight for your first couple of fights. Some gyms don't. If you are at a gym where everyone just seems to jump straight in, it can be confusing to know what to look for when you have a choice, but don't be in too much of a rush, and spend at least a little bit of time watching for a while to get a feel for who is on the mat and what they are capable of.

If you can get an upper belt to roll with you, bonus. Even better is an upper belt which is a woman, and best is an upper belt who is a woman and smaller in stature. If you are fortunate enough to have someone like this agree to roll with you, realize that these people are the treasures of our sport. They are tough enough to have made it through years of being bashed by larger aggressors. Their technique is usually very advanced, as they have, generally speaking, less reserves of strength and mass like a large, lumbering male white belt.

Treat them carefully, although they will likely beat the shit out of you; try not to be too clumsy. A knee wrongly placed can put someone like this out. If you move slowly and carefully and place their safety above yours, they will learn to trust you and can fast-track your learning with many tricks, tips, and techniques that may have taken them years to work out at great physical cost. Set your ego aside, for the more they tap you, the quicker you will learn the correct reactions, the intricacies of balance and control.

But most likely, it will be months before you even catch the attention of a person like this. You will be in a large pool of the rest of the white belt beginners for a while. Try and form a friendship with someone who has similar attributes to yours;. same sort of height and roughly the same weight. Basically, another you. You need a blank canvas partner to grow with. The two of you will learn together.

This should be someone who has about the same schedule as you so that you can train with them regularly. As you develop, the two of you will enter an arms race, growing methods of attack and then mirroring defenses together so that as one advances, the other keeps pace. A human arms race that forces both of you to continually improve as you find ways to outsmart each other, eventually learning to volley long chains of body movement together that you serve back and forth like a tennis match.

Size and sex

In general, you wouldn't say no after a while to most people that offered you a match. I can give you some guidelines, but just like everywhere, you are the one looking after your own safety. I will also add that a younger person might not have that many side effects from being injured other than an inconvenience for a few weeks. If you are the sole provider in your household, you absolutely should be using that as a factor to determine who to roll with. Still don't know what I mean? The giant mid 20's Purple belt competitor might be a worse choice for you than the smaller Brown belt who has two kids. Regardless of belt level, someone more similar to you is usually an ideal training partner. It will take about six months after you start rolling to begin to identify the difference between people who want to train consistently with you and people who want to consistently try to injure you for the win. There's room on the mat for all levels. If someone is bringing too much mass, aggression, or intention to the mat, you can avoid them actively and roll with someone else with no shame. After all, if you get injured, you might not be able to pick up your little kids. You might not be able to do your job, and put food on the table. That is a higher responsibility than being able to say you beat someone at training and have to pay the (always physical, sometimes financial) high cost of injury.

Your Training Partners and Your Ego

A large factor in making the above decision is your relationship with your own ego. Your ego (especially if you are a man, but no one is immune) can get you in a lot of trouble. One of the best whole-life improvements from jiu-jitsu is what it can do for your ego. After all, it just isn't possible to hold the worldview that you are a badass if you keep getting beaten at practice. Once you enter the water here, you see how quickly a smaller person can drown you with technique. Some of the most dangerous people in the gym are smaller skilled people who often have a very innocuous appearance out on the street. When you discover how deceiving looks can be, you start to assess the world according to the actual potential threat, and you stop making the assumption that you are always capable of beating someone in a fight "because you see red when the chips are down."

It's said that success is the ability to recover quickly from repeated failure, and that is one of the not-so-secret secrets of jiu-jitsu. The quicker and more often you tap out over a longer period, the steeper your improvement curve will be. It's crucial that you quickly accept that someone who has better technique will beat your technique. They may not be strong enough or fast enough to beat you full stop, but you are not at practice to develop physical attributes, although you will. You are there to develop technique. So concentrate on technique and not muscling your way out of a position. If you are very strong, to begin with, try to use as little strength as possible and as much technique to win. Your only real goal when you roll is to be able to come back tomorrow. It doesn't matter if you won, if you went so hard that you won't be able to walk right for a couple of days.

Strong Like Bull

Ever heard of old man strength?

Do you remember being a kid and trying to drag your mother or grandfather after you to get somewhere? Sometimes they sped up, but usually, they just kept the same pace, and you were forced to just settle in for the ride. They were pacing themselves. They knew they had a long day ahead of them, with many more requests to hurry, lift you up, or buy something. There's a lesson there.

After a little while at your new gym, it's really likely that someone will compliment you on your "Old Man Strength," especially if you've been a tradesman or been skilled labor for the last 20+ years. Maybe you really are strong. But very likely, you are more patient than they are and just moving much more slowly, conserving energy and strength like a character's power bar building up on a video game. Saving the torque for just the right moment instead of spraying it everywhere. You're old enough to have the perspective to know that the one correct move, however small, doesn't need much power. It takes younger students years to learn the attribute of patience that you may already have.

Further to this, older athletes should be more focused on developing their defense first. This isn't where a younger jiteiro starts. They want the flashy flying triangle or the punishing electric chair for their opponent and often blindly focus on submissions before they have developed a solid defense. This gives us a distinct advantage because, by now in life, we should have developed the patience required to allow someone to exhaust themselves against our defenses before coming out of our shell for an attack.

Almost no one in a bjj gym works on their cardio outside actually practicing jiu-jitsu. Cardio, strength endurance, and flexibility are the areas where an older athlete can gain a tactical advantage by working on these things outside practice and bringing this advantage back to the mat with us.

The technique is the final advantage we will have to develop to push the boundaries of equality with our younger teammates. As an old guy, you have likely spent your entire life up to this point learning how to be really good at something. Maybe you have been in your job for years and worked out all the tricks to make it more efficient. Maybe you are a hunter or angler and can bring the ability to think like prey. Maybe you're a parent and accustomed to working out moves a few steps ahead of your kids, so you don't get surprised often and can anticipate an opponent's moves.

You might not have any concrete skills at all that directly translate to jiu-jitsu, but you likely have spent more time learning things than younger players. That, too, is an advantage because learning how to learn is a skill.

The Notes

At least in the beginning, you should be taking some kind of notes. When you start, everything will be confusing. The best way to find your way in the wilderness is to observe and make notes. This can be an as low-tech as an actual paper notebook. Obviously, you can use your phone, a tablet, or a laptop. Ask your professor for permission if you want to take a video of the class with your phone or an action camera, as this is intellectual property, and many gyms have their own video content online for profit or as member-only content.

I started with a paper notebook; for the first year or so, I would sit on the edge of the mat or in the car at the end of practice and write down as much as I remembered of the day's technique. Sometimes if I had a question, I'd message a quick question to my professor later at home when I was revising my sloppy notes from practice or the day before. I actually remember having a bit of trouble writing at the end of practices back then, as my forearms would be cooked and my hands trembling. Eventually, I transitioned online. I don't take as many notes for individual classes now; in theory, a couple of years of practice would make you familiar with all but the latest techniques (which are constantly evolving at a higher level). For many of the entries I make now (in the app Evernote), I can keyword search for the specific move, so if I want all the information I have on the Bow and Arrow choke, I can use a simple word search. Any sort of cloud storage will be fine, and my online hoarding of jiu-jitsu material has spread into other pools, on my google drive, in dropbox, and access or subscriptions to various websites.

Sometimes my entries are now more conceptual, maybe about a move someone has written about or a list of sequences. More often now, I'll see something I want to save, a tip that I think applies specifically to my game, a stretching technique or a video, and sometimes a recipe for training food or something like that. I use the free version of Evernote and find it works brilliantly for typing something straight in, copying directly from the web (following your favorite athletes and coaches on social media will yield some amazing material). Recently, I've started using a daily paper journal, called the Mono Journal, and it's really a great tool, I recommend it as well.

Old Injuries

So we've got some road miles at our age. Hopefully well used and not abused, but accidents do happen. If you're looking at this sport as a potential pastime in the first place, I'd say you were probably someone who is not totally risk averse. You might be the sort of person with motorcycle or soccer injuries; maybe you were a tree climber, rodeo cowboy, or college football player. Regardless of how you got any injury, you may suddenly find yourself at the front door of a gym thinking, "This is crazy; what if I hurt myself again?".

Personally, when I started jits, I had a C5/6 ruptured disc and had childhood surgery on my right ACL. At the end of my first practice, I told the coach how much I enjoyed myself but expressed concern for my neck. His response was where my personal responsibility began, and his ended. "Are you sure this is the right thing for you to be doing?" he asked me, but it was too late by then. I was hooked. But there is a clear division of responsibility. I took on the entire responsibility of my well-being on the mat. He was not responsible if I was permanently injured.

This hopefully will never be an issue but make no mistake, it is dangerous, you must sign a waiver holding the gym harmless, and it will remain your ultimate responsibility. In my first year, an ex-ball player, nicknamed "Captain America" for his endless reserves of power, strength, and recovery) took a huge hit to the head and neck and nearly became paralyzed.

Ironically, the news he brought back from many months of rehab was the proud announcement that the doctors said, but for the strength and flexibility he had gained as attributes from jiu-jitsu, he would surely have been permanently paralyzed.

To be honest, I had never thought ten years prior that I'd be able to do anything like this. In my mind, it was totally out of the question. My neurosurgeon (who I never did let operate on my neck, he lost me at "we go in through the throat!") told me to be very careful with the rest of my life, or there was a chance of paralysis.

My intro to martial arts was a karate school I enrolled my young children in. I watched all of them grow inside the karate program, and when they were old enough that the youngest was finally dressing for practice, I jumped in with them. I did karate with them for five years, and my balance, strength, and especially flexibility in my neck grew. This elevated my confidence, but I became unsatisfied with the lack of contact. The school we were at emphasized demonstration karate.

They called it XMA, and the emphasis was not on actual defense but on showmanship. I became increasingly unsatisfied with the group of adults I trained with, some my own age, but much younger who had no interest in actual contact and just wanted to stay in shape and dress up in pajamas. Most of our class time was spent demonstrating and practicing 'Kata,' the semi-formal dances that are collectively a laundry list of all the techniques of your school. It looks pretty cool. It has limited effectiveness until you have drilled the Kata so many times the order of the dance links all the moves together, and you are able to magically use the right move in a conflict someday. In theory.

Finally, one day my belt level was practicing forward rolls (by this time, I was spending more time eye rolling), and on the other side of the mat, the three black belts were practicing arm bars. This looked fun. More fun than what I was doing. But I wouldn't be able to practice arm bars for three more belts, with my work schedule, that could take years. It was that simple. I couldn't take it anymore; I went home that night and found the three BJJ gyms close to me and rang one for a trial. I pulled everyone out of karate the following week and have been doing BJJ since.

You will find very few medical professionals who will tell you they think Brazilian Jiu-Jitsu is a good idea at all. Quite the opposite. If you take up this sport unless you see a doctor who is also involved in combat sport, almost to a (wo)man, they will tell you to stop doing jiu-jitsu every time you visit the office to be healed. They aren't wrong. But in Jiu-Jitsu, you do take some pride in your battle wounds. You can't help it. There is a grisly satisfaction in showing up to work with the rare black eye or visible abrasion and knowing that the people around you would be crippled or killed in personal combat while you might come away pretty well.

Knee and ankle braces

If you have old joint injuries, they will play up from time to time. You have to develop a game that protects the worst of them. An example would never be letting your arm get raised above your head if you have shoulder issues. 100% you need to communicate to your partner that you might tap early. Tell them your right shoulder or left knee or both ankles have old injuries, and they should concentrate attacks on the good side.

I sometimes carry a light knee pad in my bag in case my knee feels dickey. If you were a high school or college wrestler, you are used to wearing a knee pad on the leg you shoot in with. Some wrestlers wear both knee pads to not give away a preferred side. In BJJ, you wear knee pads under your pants if you wear them, so not as big of a tell. If you wear a knee brace, it should not have any metal or hard hinges, pinch points, etc., or anything that could be a danger to others. I like both an Asics brand gel pad and a simple drugstore noname brand neoprene one, depending on the level of protection I feel like I need. Recently, I purchased a Bauerfeind brace, costly but undoubtedly better. I use it only when I feel like I need additional support or to signal repeatedly to a partner that I have a bad knee that should be looked after. Personally, I think wearing a brace all the time would make my knee weaker. Instead, I choose to put some time into things that strengthen and make it more resilient, like low-impact walking and yoga.

If you decide to go the nogi route, it is quite common for students at schools like 10th Planet to wear ankle braces because of the prevalence of leglocks, heel hooks, toe holds, etc.

I have also grappled people who wear shoulder, elbow, and wrist braces. I had a training partner for a long time who wore elbow and wrist braces on the same side arm and had no ability to grip that side. I just attacked the other side and let him work his bad arm as much as possible.

△

Chapter 5: A Fortune in Tape

Especially in the beginning, you may get to the end of practice and be unable to make a fist or close your fingers into one. Your wrists and forearms will likely burn, and you may have jammed a finger or two, especially the joints of the smaller ones. Have a look at the finger joints of someone who has practiced for a long time, and you might notice that all their finger joints are swollen like little balloons. Neither my wedding ring nor my university class ring has fit for some years.

At this point, most people discover tape. Some people take 20 minutes to tape up their hands, and it looks like they're wearing gloves to practice. There are special techniques for taping fingers, but IMO, the best way to care for your fingers is not to ask too much of them. I taped for a while when I started, and I still carry tape in my bag for injuries, but the best way to make your fingers and grips last longer is two things, and they're pretty simple:

1. LET GO. Seems obvious. If something (like sweaty canvas) keeps getting ripped from your super tight grips, and that is why they get hurt....stop doing that. But don't give up on your grips. When a grip you have is challenged by force, let go and immediately grab that grip (or something close to it) again when unchallenged. I will mention that grip-intensive guards and moves should

probably be screened out of your game. Spider Guard, I am pointing a mashed-up finger at you.

2. Make BIGGER grips. The issue with having your grips on someone's gi broken again and again is that they are so small and tight. Your hand is curled up in a tiny ball under a huge amount of tension. This can lead to exhaustion and cramping and ultimately cause the kind of damage I'm talking about above. So open your hand and make a bigger grip. Here are some substitutions you can easily make. Instead of the collar grip, grab the back of the neck or hook your hand over the traps, maybe palming the shoulder blade if you can reach it. Alternatively, maybe get an underhook at the armpit. Instead of a sleeve, encircle the forearm just at the bump of the wrist. For extra effectiveness, turn their entire hand away from your body anytime you can. A hand can only grab what it is facing. Instead of a pant grip, grab or C grip the whole ankle. You get the idea.

3. Make YOUR OWN grips. By this, I mean grab yourself in a way that makes a strong grip but allows you to force multiply. Maybe you palm your own thigh to keep an armbar. Grab your own lapel. Use both hands, palm to palm, around the neck to break posture, or around the body to throw.

△

Chapter 6: Heal Yourself

Repair

Since I started practicing, I've suffered a range of injuries, both minor and 'major.' Mostly jammed fingers, sore toes, sore neck, muscle pulls, rib injuries, and hyperextended joints. The worst was probably the MCL of my right knee, which was a grade 2 tear. Bad enough to put me on my ass for a week and light duty for six weeks. No jiu-jitsu for a couple of months. Once you get used to the beatings, you'll shrug off minor injuries. You should be able to take more serious injuries in stride, or you are risking more than you should. Be careful! It isn't more important to win every match than it is to be able to work, feed your family, or pick your kids up.

Movement, not rest

Pretty much everyone who ever did high school sports has heard the acronym **RICE**. In this context, it stands for **R**est, **I**ce, **C**ompression, and **E**levation. Published in 1996 by Dr. Jim and Phil Wharton, The Wharton's Stretch Book was one of the first advocates that recovery after injury is improved with *movement*, not rest.

In the book, they put forward the acronym **MICE** to replace **RICE**, where **R**est is replaced with **M**ovement. The

Whartons advocated that once injury is confirmed, and there is no fracture or catastrophic injury; movement is better than rest, to treat an injury. They encouraged immediate (but moderate) restoration of an active range of motion, with the gradual introduction of fully functional activity. They note that total inactivity shuts the muscle down. Blood flow is then restricted, and tissue atrophy follows. In contrast, activity improves blood flow, which brings oxygen and removes metabolic waste. Unlike the cardiovascular system, which has a dedicated pump in the form of the heart muscle, or the respiratory system, which has the lungs as pumps, the lymphatic system has no central pump of its own. For this reason, the fluid tends to move comparatively slowly in the body; lymph fluid is pushed along its path as we breathe or move. The movement of lymph in the body plays a crucial role in the healing process of an injury.

Lymph is a clear fluid that circulates through the lymphatic system, removing waste and toxins from the body's tissues. When an injury occurs, the lymphatic system goes into overdrive to help remove damaged cells and promote the growth of new, healthy tissue. By transporting these waste products away from the injury site, the lymphatic system helps to reduce swelling and prevent infection. Additionally, the movement of lymph helps to deliver oxygen and nutrients to the area, which is necessary for the body to heal itself. Without the proper flow of lymph, an injury would take longer to heal and could become infected. So, the movement of lymph is an essential aspect of the body's self-healing mechanism and helps to get us back to our daily activities as quickly and safely as possible.

But maybe not even Ice?

It might even be that icing should be reconsidered. Many authorities agree that ice can actually slow and, in a lot of cases, even retard the healing process. There are studies in the recent history published in The American Journal of Sports Medicine (2004), The British Journal of Sports Medicine (2012), the Journal of Strength and Conditioning Research/National Strength and Conditioning Association (2013), and the Journal of Emergency Medicine (2008) among others that agree that there is no conclusive proof that ice heals faster. In fact, some of studies show that it actually retards healing. Cooling the area of injury can slow the removal of damaged tissue and reduce the oxygenation of the healthy tissue surrounding it. In extreme cases, it can kill the tissue. This is called frostbite.

What they all found was that the inflammatory response is needed to initiate healing. So if you habitually take ibuprofen or other non-steroidal anti-inflammatories

(NSAID), you may temporarily feel better, but you will actually inhibit the healing process.

Compression and Elevation

There isn't a lot of evidence to either confirm or refute the benefit of compression or elevation to recovery either, although they have long been represented as being equal in importance to icing.

Compression and elevation

Evidence to confirm or refute the benefit of injury recovery is scanty and difficult to perform. The influence of a placebo effect is suspected. A pilot study on the effect of compression socks on recovery from a five-kilometer sprint did confirm that those who believed the socks would help did do better than those who were skeptical of their benefit. I have used in the past a calf muscle pump for muscular soreness. Walk as soon as you are able, but make sure you schedule enough time during the recovery period to get around. What I mean is that you should be walking much more slowly than usual, avoiding any limping or hopping. You should concentrate on making your stride slow but perfect as you recover, placing each step carefully, especially in the beginning of your recovery phase, to heal efficiently and completely. This strategy should include scheduling extra time to arrive and leave appointments or meetings.

The emotional cost of injury

The emotional cost of injury may be moderated by permission to move immediately. It starts with a range of motion and walking. Cross-training can maintain fitness and supplement strengthening drills. Low-intensity practices start soon, with a gradual progression to full participation when sufficient strength and agility are realized.

What I do now

Excluding of course a major fracture, spinal cord injury, or catastrophic injury, I like to get moving post-injury and do a range of motion exercises as soon as possible.

- For foot and ankle injuries, draw the alphabet with your toes.
- For knees: stationary biking with low tension. Low speed, longer easy sessions.
- For shoulder injuries: pendulums, pole walking, and Nordic ski.
- For neck pain: rows and ellipse.
- For back pain: walking, swimming, and yoga.
- For lower limb fractures: water running and seated weights.

- For upper limb fractures: walking and the recumbent bike.

I minimize the use of braces, splints, or slings and recommend visiting a physiotherapist to maintain the range of motion of surrounding joints for casted fractures.

Ice works great immediately after injury for pain and to control initial swelling. Use compression after a few days if it works for you. Also calf pump exercises, walking, and cross-training. Light strength and agility exercises can start right away. Resume training and practices as soon as you feel strong enough, with gradual easing back to full function over time. This is a great time to focus on the accuracy of your movements, not the speed. When it's time to ease back into training, younger kids at the club can be great training partners, if you're involved in the kid's program. They are lighter and the forces used will be much less. Additionally, you will have to move slowly and accurately to not injure them. Great for getting your form and movements back.

Movement, not rest.

Options: Find other options for cross-training, train around your injury sensibly.

Vary rehabilitation with strength, balance, and agility drills.

Ease back to activity as early as possible for emotional strength.

△

Chapter 7: Diet

When you are a kid, you can eat fast food an hour before working out and run up and down the court with no problem. You might puke, but no long-lasting damage will have been done, and you'll do it again next week if you're hungry. An athlete who is in their 20's thinks nothing of staying out past midnight drinking and hitting the open mat Saturday afternoon. I hope you know that won't work for you now. There are a large number of older jits guys out there that swear beer is a perfect training beverage, but if I'm being honest, although I did like to drink to excess when I was younger, it has almost no place in my life now. There are so few hours that I can legit get to practice without displacing something else in my life that I'm loath to waste any of my training time feeling crap because I drank the night before.

Many, many books have been written on the topic of diets. There are some supposed jiu-jitsu specific diets out there. All diets to lose weight work the same way, through calorie restriction. If you start putting fewer calories into yourself because you are limited to eating only potatoes, or because you decide to eat only intermittently in a 'window,' or you only eat meat or only eat vegetables, or for that matter bugs, you will lose weight as your body uses up excess stores of energy. All of these diets reduce the number of calories you take on board. But at some point, most people go back to eating the way they had, or they slack off at some point and start eating shit again. It's not rocket science. If you are getting a good night's sleep (8 hrs), moderate exercise, and eating reasonably, you will eventually reach a weight that suits you perfectly. This can take some time depending on how long you've prioritised eating instead of exercising!

Eat More Protein, Fewer Refined Carbs

Along with the shift to eating more plants and fewer animals, athletes over 40 should be moderately increasing their intake of protein and making an effort to reduce the intake of concentrated carbohydrate sources. You don't have to go low carb or swear off bread and pasta, but it is important to understand that highly concentrated sources of carbohydrate energy make it easy to consume way more calories than you need or intend to eat.

Concentrated carbohydrate sources are great around the times you are actually exercising, but cutting back on them in the rest of your diet helps reduce overall caloric intake. When you combine the advice to consume more plants and fewer animals with the advice to consume fewer concentrated carbohydrate sources, you naturally end up with the recommendation to eat more fruits and vegetables.

Some people advocate rounding out your energy intake almost entirely with fat, but athletes in their 40s should instead aim to consume 1.5 - 1.7 grams of protein per kilogram of body weight per day, maybe as high as up to 2 g/kg/day. This still leaves plenty of room in an athlete's diet for fats and oils but also helps ensure you're getting enough protein to support your muscle mass, immune health, and recovery needs.

△

Chapter 8: Build a Better Machine

How's your cardio?

You're about to fight for your life.

Possibly you ran at some point recreationally. After doing that for a while, maybe you ran some smaller races, maybe a marathon. The common factor is a race run for time. If you are going to run to supplement your cardio for jiu-jitsu, at this age, you are not racing. You should not be using an easy cardio session for sprinting.

In fact, depending on how good your hips, knees, and ankles are, maybe you shouldn't be running at all. I spoke to a friend recently who was a career military man. During his active service training life, he was accustomed to "rucking" long distances with a heavy pack. At 50, his knees are totally blown. His shoulders are wrecked. "So, what do you do for exercise now?" I ask him.

"Last week, I did 10K with a pack", he said, "It was pretty easy."

"How do your knees feel?" I said, not believing what I was hearing.

"Yeah, they hurt; I've scheduled another surgery for April."

SERIOUSLY!? If what you are doing is causing or has caused serious injury and the need for surgery (multiple surgeries?!?), maybe it's time to ask if you should keep doing it. He would be much better served by a short, easy daily walk than a single knee-wrecking event once or twice a month. Remember, recovery is about getting the joints moving. The cardio is a bonus. Jiu-jitsu is a sport that is best learned by being consistent. Injuries interrupt training. Prioritise not being injured, and you will go much further in a shorter time frame.

Almost any off the mat supplemental exercise needs to be constantly reviewed to make sure you're rebuilding, not further destroying your ability to train. Activities like a daily walk, or an easy bike ride. The area I live in has a long, cold, rainy winter. I struggled with running outside for a few years, but honestly, the impact on my hips and knees wasn't manageable and affected my ability to get onto the mat. For my 50th birthday, I bought myself a really nice stationary bike. It's in my living room, and it's really efficient to spend 20 minutes a day on it to catch up on the news or watch a show. I just roll it over in front of the tv. Cardio exercise in the morning has a number of extended metabolic benefits beyond just burning calories during the workout. Doing cardio in the morning on an empty stomach has been shown to increase fat burning and metabolism throughout the day, as the body continues to use stored fat as fuel. Additionally, morning cardio can also help regulate insulin levels, leading to better glucose metabolism and improved energy levels. Furthermore, exercising in the morning can also lead to a boost in mood and cognitive function, helping to set a positive tone for the rest of the day. Finally, like making your bed, if you go out in the world and the day is a complete loss, you can always reflect on the fact that at least you got it done today.

Yoga is an amazing off sport activity, and for a time I was doing yoga every day I wasn't rolling. It's a fantastic way to gain flexibility while rebuilding your joints and protecting range of motion. I maintained a membership at a local yoga studio for a couple of years, and found that consistant yoga classes actually allowed me to add more jiu jitsu to the schedule. But you don't have to attend a class. Especially in the last few years there is a huge amount of online content and you can find top instruction on Youtube. There are private instructors if you find you can't make a class schedule work for you. Some jiu jitsu gyms have yoga programs and instructors and if this is the case I'd encourage you to give it a try.

Strength training

Metabolism follows muscle mass, so maintaining muscle mass becomes increasingly important as we get older. Strength training also helps maintain bone density, which is particularly important for athletes with a long history in non-weight-bearing sports like cycling and swimming or people who were sedentary in early adulthood and have become more active in recent years. Joint health is a third reason to add or increase strength training – in case you need another. There's an old saying: "motion is lotion" regarding joint health. Incorporating a variety of strength training movements helps keep your joints moving in a wide range of motion and applies stress at novel angles, which helps maintain the strength of connective tissues (tendons and ligaments).

Exercise More Consistently, Less Specifically

Improving an athlete's performance in a very specific activity is a unique challenge. If you want to win an event, your training needs to be very specific to the demands of that event. Specific to our demographic group. However, it is important for older athletes to prioritize consistent general activity over sport-specific activity. Even sport-specific athletes benefit from diversifying their ability to participate in a wider range of activities. If you're a runner, you can still be a runner, but adding strength training and cycling, and even bouldering or stick-and-ball sports to your lifestyle will help you have better general fitness. If you're a wrestler, it's even more important to diversify so you can participate in more weight-bearing activities. The point is to increase your options so you can exercise consistently, no matter what activity or equipment is available. Make sure you can always do something; don't worry as much about exactly what that something is. Jiu-jitsu will constantly be serving you with new challenges, and you will very likely injure parts of your body that will affect your training modality. The responsibility to continue pushing forward is yours. A knee injury doesn't affect your upper body. Likewise, a wrist injury should not prevent you from keeping your cardio on track. Be wary against using the excuse of an injury to completely stop training. The longer you take a break at our age, the harder it becomes to get back to training. One excuse becomes four in a row, and before you know it, you haven't been back for weeks. The secret at our age is to STAY in shape once you get there. Otherwise you'll have to fight the hardest part of the battle all over again when it's time to get back to training consistantly after an injury.

△

Chapter 9: Inflammation and Supplements

Inflammation, Diet, and Supplements

A little bit of inflammation contributes to healing, but when inflammation becomes chronic, it can trigger disease processes. Chronic inflammation can damage your heart, brain, and other organs, and it plays a role in nearly every major illness, including cancer, heart disease, Alzheimer's disease, and depression.

An anti-inflammatory diet can help to reduce inflammation in your body by avoiding processed foods, eating mostly plant-based foods, and including foods rich in omega-3 fatty acids. Eating more fish, fruits and vegetables, nuts and seeds, whole grains, and healthy fats like olive oil can help reduce inflammation. Avoiding foods high in saturated fats, like processed meats and high-fat dairy products, can also help.

An anti-inflammatory diet also includes foods with omega-3 fatty acids, like salmon, tuna, walnuts, and flaxseeds. Other foods that are beneficial for an anti-inflammatory diet include raw honey, olive oil, green tea, and herbs like turmeric and ginger. Additionally, it is important to limit processed and refined foods, sugar, alcohol, and red meat.

One approach that can be incredibly effective is utilizing a combination of saunas, ice baths, and cryotherapy. The contrast between the hot and cold temperatures triggers the production of heat shock proteins, which have been shown to have anti-inflammatory effects. By incorporating these practices into my routine, I've noticed a significant reduction in soreness and an overall improvement in my recovery time.

Supplements can be beneficial for some people, but it's important to consult with a physician before taking any.
Caffeine is known to have anti-inflammatory effects, which can help reduce the inflammation caused by various medical conditions. Studies have shown that caffeine consumption can reduce inflammation and oxidative stress, which can help reduce pain, swelling, and other symptoms associated with inflammation. However, it's important to note that too much caffeine can have the opposite effect and can even worsen inflammation, so it's important to be mindful of your caffeine intake. I never consume any caffeine before training for two main reasons. First, I find that no matter what the amount or when I take it, it often results in painful foot cramps during practice, likely from it contributing to dehydration. The second is that caffeine makes me have a lot more energy, and I've found that

personally, it makes me more aggressive during matches, which has a knock-on effect resulting in more injury. Simply put, I find it much easier to keep a conservative attitude during matches without caffeine.

Turmeric is a great supplement for improving overall health and promoting inflammation reduction. Turmeric is a spice that comes from a flowering plant in the ginger family. It is commonly used in Indian and Asian cooking and is known for its vibrant yellow color and earthy, slightly bitter flavor profile. It is also known for its many health benefits, such as its anti-inflammatory, antioxidant and anti-cancer properties. Turmeric can be found in most grocery stores either in its whole root form or as a ground powder. Below is a recipe for a hot drink that can be made from it.

Golden Latte

Ingredients:

- 1 cup almond milk (or your favorite dairy-free milk)
- 1 teaspoon turmeric powder
- 1 teaspoon ground ginger
- 1 tablespoon honey (or maple syrup for a vegan version)
- 1 teaspoon coconut oil
- Pinch of black pepper
- Optional: a pinch of cinnamon

Instructions:

1. Heat the almond milk over medium heat until hot but not boiling.
2. Add the turmeric, ginger, honey, coconut oil, and black pepper and whisk until combined.
3. Pour the golden latte into a cup or mug

If desired, add a pinch of cinnamon for a little extra flavor.

Magnesium is another great supplement for improving energy and aiding in muscle recovery. Magnesium is a mineral that is essential for good health and has many important functions in the body. It helps to regulate blood pressure and blood sugar levels and plays a role in muscle and nerve function. It also helps to keep bones strong and helps the body to produce energy. Magnesium can be found in many foods, such as dark leafy greens, fish, beans, nuts, and avocados. Taking a magnesium supplement can also be beneficial for those who do not get enough from their diet. I've found that I benefit from a couple of magnesium capsules taken at night. It helps me sleep and can have amazing results in reducing muscle soreness and preventing cramps, especially for me in hot weather. More is not always better; you will find there is an upper limit to how much you can absorb. A possible side effect of too much supplemental magnesium is a pretty aggressive laxative effect, so adjust your dosage with caution.

Testosterone is essential for building muscle, increasing strength, and improving endurance. Achieving and maintaining a healthy testosterone level for athletes is important for optimal performance. To reach and maintain an optimal level, athletes should focus on getting sufficient sleep, eating a balanced diet with plenty of protein, reducing stress, and exercising regularly. Supplementation can also be beneficial, but it is important to consult with a healthcare professional first to ensure the supplements are safe and appropriate for your needs. I find that my natural Testosterone level is high enough, and as such I choose not to add it into the mix. Testosterone supplementation can have both positive and negative effects on the body. On the positive side, testosterone supplementation can help increase muscle mass, improve bone density, increase energy levels and libido, and enhance overall well-being. However, there are also potential negative side effects, including cardiovascular risks, prostate problems, testosterone abuse, hormonal imbalances, and liver damage. Additionally, testosterone supplementation can cause unwanted side effects such as acne, mood swings, and aggressive behavior. It's important to keep in mind that testosterone supplementation should only be used under the guidance of a physician and after a thorough evaluation of the individual's health and hormone levels, and the potential benefits and risks should be carefully considered before beginning treatment.

Foods that are known to help boost testosterone production include eggs, oily fish, nuts and seeds, full-fat dairy products, beef, beans, lentils, and dark, leafy greens. Additionally, some studies suggest that vitamin D, zinc, and magnesium may also play a role in testosterone production, so it's important to include foods like mushrooms, fortified cereals, and dairy products that are rich in these vitamins and minerals. Additionally, staying active and avoiding stress can also help promote healthy testosterone production.

Creatine can be a great supplement for older athletes, as it helps to increase muscle strength and power output. Studies have also shown that it can help to reduce fatigue and increase energy levels. It's important to note that creatine can cause water retention and bloating, so it's important to be aware of this possible side effect. It's best to start with a lower dose and work up if needed. Make sure to check with a doctor before taking any supplements. It’s generally agreed that Creatine takes several weeks to load to an effective level in the body.

As with any of the advice given in this book, consult with your physician to advise for your specific situation.

△

Chapter 10: Old Guy Rules for Rolling

Overview of Priorities when Rolling

1. Avoid injury – This is the most important thing to remember when rolling. If you don't get injured, you can keep training. If you can keep training, you will get better at jiu-jitsu. I know. It sounds simple. It's harder than you think. To help avoid injury while rolling, focus on playing a defensive game. Instead of trying to overpower your opponent by matching strength, look for opportunities to anticipate their moves and counter them. Use defensive techniques such as blocking, parrying, or evading to keep your opponent from scoring points or advancing position. Be mindful of how you execute your moves and keep your body in a controlled and balanced position. Any win you might get in the gym by working outside your safe boundaries will not be worth it in the long run and can affect your ability to train consistently. Injury at our age does not have to be a specific one. If it is a very hot day and you redline yourself several times in practice, it will take several days for a full recovery. You may train more efficiently by going

70-80% on these days so that you can train every day in hot weather, instead of having to wait several days for full recovery. Cold weather does not seem to have the same effect on me, but your mileage may vary.

2. Surviving while conserving energy to fight back or escape - Be mindful of your energy level and use it wisely in order to stay safe. Limit movement and conserve energy whenever possible. You don't need to be tense and struggling all the time. If there is no point in resisting the position you find yourself in, relax. Actually, think about what you need to do to escape. Wait for your opponent to move and create openings for you, rather than forcing them yourself and telegraphing your intention. Most upper belts will allow you to work slowly in the right direction to free yourself. That is not to say they will let you become free, but if you're doing the right thing, they may encourage you or offer suggestions when the match finishes.
3. Rest and take breaks when possible. Take a few moments to catch your breath and regain your energy. The coach will encourage everyone to roll every round. Try to do this, but be realistic about your ability. You don't have to win every match. Sometimes when you're tired, just not losing, if you

can complete a match having escaped, or being able to hold out for the whole round without being submitted, are all ways to keep rolling without giving up. Remember to tap. TAP TAP TAP! Verbally and by tapping your partner, not yourself or the mat. This will keep you from having something snapped off by accident. Don't just look to rest between rounds; also rest within the round if you can. If you're in a stable position, relax and catch your breath while holding your opponent at bay.

4. Using strategy, guile, and technique to offset a younger opponent's strength, speed, and mass. Almost without exception, younger athletes are more impatient than you. They will leave huge openings, miss important grips, and skip steps or cut corners to try and finish a move. Every time they exercise impatience is an opportunity for an older grappler who has been waiting for the right moment to seize it. Marcelo Garcia's Elbow Push sweep is a great example of this; lying in wait for a small opportunity to capitalize on.

Whether you're looking for a way to start or continue training as you get older, the answers are really pretty simple. It's about prioritizing and setting habits well that support following the following guidelines.

- Get adequate sleep - Getting adequate sleep is essential for our overall health and well-being. Aim to get between 7-9 hours of sleep each night. Make sure to create a comfortable environment for yourself and reduce distractions like electronics, background noise, and light. Additionally, try to have a consistent bedtime and waketime schedule, even on weekends. If you have trouble falling asleep, try some relaxation techniques like deep breathing, progressive muscle relaxation, or light stretching. Read a book but avoid screens one hour prior to bedtime. You should not consume any caffeine ten hours prior to bedtime
- Hydrate constantly and replace lost minerals when necessary - Staying hydrated is incredibly important for your overall health and well-being. It's recommended that you drink at least eight glasses of water a day to keep your body hydrated. Additionally, it's important to replace lost minerals when necessary. Eating foods rich in minerals, such as fruits and vegetables, can help you replenish essential nutrients and minerals. Additionally, you may also want to consider taking at least a daily

multivitamin supplement to ensure you get the necessary minerals your body needs.

- Eat to be lean and healthy - The key to achieving this is to make sure you're eating nutritious foods that will fill you up and keep you satisfied, such as lean proteins, fresh fruits and vegetables, and healthy fats. Your diet should heavily favor fruits and vegetables, with clean proteins making up only a third overall of your intake. It's also important to practice mindful eating - listen to your body's cues and don't overindulge. Finally, make sure you're getting enough exercise to keep your body fit and healthy.
- Supplemental Training for strength and function - Resistance training is a great way to improve muscle strength and function, as well as balance and coordination. Additionally, plyometric exercises can help to improve power and agility. Other activities, such as yoga and Pilates, can be useful for building strength and flexibility. Bodyweight exercises such as planks and squats can be effective for building strength and improving functional abilities. Compound lifts such as Deadlifts and Squats are excellent exercises to add to additional exercise plans.

- Consistent, easy outdoor activity for passive recovery – In addition to the stationary bike, I try and walk outside 4-5 times a week. Walking or jogging outside is a great way to get some passive recovery. It's easy to fit into your daily routine and can be done almost anywhere. Make sure to wear comfortable shoes, dress appropriately for the weather, and bring water, so you stay hydrated. Additionally, consider adding a little variety to your routine by exploring different paths and parks in your area. This can not only help keep your recovery enjoyable but also offer a variety of scenery to help keep you motivated.
- Being part of social and support groups - This is incredibly valuable for anyone practicing jiu-jitsu. Not only does it provide a sense of community and belonging, but it also encourages the continued practice of the sport. Jiu-jitsu can be a challenging and demanding sport, and having a group of like-minded individuals who share the same passion and goals can be incredibly motivating.

In addition to the social benefits, being part of a jiu-jitsu community can also help identify common problems and solutions in the demographic. For example, many practitioners may struggle with specific techniques or experience injuries or other setbacks. Being part of a community can allow individuals to share their experiences and learn from each other's successes and challenges. Additionally, members of a jiu-jitsu community may have access to resources and information that can help them overcome these obstacles and continue to improve their skills.

Overall, the value of being part of a social and support group in jiu-jitsu cannot be overstated. It provides a sense of camaraderie, motivation, and support that can make all the difference in a practitioner's journey. It also allows individuals to identify common problems and solutions in the demographic, creating a more knowledgeable and connected community. I've started a community like this, you can make contact with me and others like you at the Old Guy Jiu Jitsu Facebook page, or a the Oldguyjits.com website. Looking forward to connecting with you!

Conclusion

I hope I've helped get you ready to begin your practice of Brazilian jiu-jitsu. It's a great sport, filled with friendly, unique people who will make your life richer and more filled with meaning the more time you spend in this community. I truly hope this has helped you and would love to hear from you with feedback or suggestions for future edits of content.

If you've made it this far and you're regularly training, congratulations! I would love to connect with you and hear your success story.

-e-

www.ingramcontent.com/pod-product-compliance
Ingram Content Group UK Ltd.
Pitfield, Milton Keynes, MK11 3LW, UK
UKHW062258290726
14090UKWH00017B/755

9 781916 626201